WILD *at* HEART

A BAND OF BROTHERS

WILD at HEART

A BAND OF BROTHERS

DISCOVERING THE SECRET *of* A MAN'S SOUL

JOHN ELDREDGE

NASHVILLE
A Division of Thomas Nelson, Inc.
www.ThomasNelson.com

Published in Nashville, Tennessee, by Thomas Nelson, Inc.

Executive Producer: Michael S. Hyatt

Published in association with Yates & Yates, LLP, Attorneys and Counselors, Orange, California.

Unless otherwise noted, Scripture quotations are from the HOLY BIBLE: NEW INTERNATIONAL VERSION®. Copyright © 1973, 1978, 1984 by International Bible Society. Used by permission of Zondervan Publishing House. All rights reserved.

Scripture quotations noted NASB are taken from the NEW AMERICAN STANDARD BIBLE®, © Copyright The Lockman Foundation 1960, 1962, 1963, 1968, 1971, 1972, 1973, 1975, 1977. Used by permission.

Scripture quotations noted NLT are from the *Holy Bible*, New Living Translation, copyright © 1996. Used by permission of Tyndale House Publishers, Inc., Wheaton, Illinois 60189. All rights reserved.

Scripture quotations noted NKJV are from THE NEW KING JAMES VERSION. Copyright © 1979, 1980, 1982 by Thomas Nelson, Inc. Used by permission. All rights reserved.

Individual Facilitator's Guide: ISBN 1-4002-0077-6
Complete Leader's Kit: ISBN 0-7852-6278-4

Printed in the United States of America
04 05 06 07 PHX 6 5 4

CONTENTS

INTRODUCTION

Sometime around the evening of May 31, 1944, small satchels were handed out to the officers of the U.S. First Army and the British Second Army, whose combined forces would soon assault the beaches of Normandy. These were *field* officers, the men who would actually lead the greatest invasion the world has ever known. On the outside, they were ordinary men by the world's standards—farmers from Iowa, mechanics from New York, grocery store clerks from Cheshire. To these men were given the long-developed, top secret plans for the invasion and detailed maps of the coast of Normandy. Once the invasion began, the outcome of the war passed from the hands of the generals to the hands of these brave men.

And, as you remember, they performed beautifully. Years later, one army Ranger returned to the beaches with a sense of awe and wonder. "Will somebody tell me how we did this?" he asked. They did it, of course, by the grace of God. That's the whole story of the Bible, isn't it? Remarkable events accomplished by seemingly ordinary people. An aging man with a speech problem (on the lam and wanted for murder) leads the Exodus; a little shepherd boy brings down a giant with his slingshot; a disenfranchised Pharisee takes the gospel to the world. It helps me to remember that when I find myself swept up into a work of God.

I'm not being dramatic when I say that the guide you are holding at least equals, if not outweighs, the significance of those D-Day satchels. For the invasion we are now involved in serves an even greater King, against an even greater foe, for an even greater cause. To rescue men, to see them restored by Christ and released for God's kingdom, is the most desperate need of this hour. The guys you will take through this experience will never be the same again. And because of that, their wives and their children will never be the same. You are about to set off a chain reaction of redemption and healing that will tremble across churches and communities, and reverberate down through generations.

Thanks for taking on this mission.

Oh, I know—you don't quite feel up to the task. Neither do I. The good news is, you don't have to have any experience leading men to take a few guys with you on this journey. With God's help, we've created a tool in this video series that God will use to set men free. All you need to do is invite them in, provide a place for this to happen, and share your own journey as a fellow pilgrim. We'll show you how to use this tool in this *Facilitator's Guide*. All you need to do is take the plunge, and God will take care of the rest.

I have come to the conclusion that if we are really going to help men, and through them their families, their loved ones, and the world, three things have to happen. First, a man has to get his own heart back. Without that, he isn't going to make it. Second, he has to find his place in the battle. God has a call on every man's life, and nothing seems to fit until we find the role we were meant for. Third, we have to teach him how to fight. That is the mission. That is the objective. If we can accomplish that, then everything else will follow. Give a man back his heart; show him his place in the battle; teach him how to fight. That's your mission. Here's the tool to help you do it.

HOW TO USE THIS TOOL

The *Wild at Heart* video series is presented in eight parts, each about thirty-five minutes in length. Each part builds upon the others in a clear flow, a path designed to take a man on the journey he must follow to begin to get his heart back, find his place in the battle, and learn how to fight. Each part works hand in hand with the *Field Manual* for a deeper, richer experience. Remember, what we're after here is irreversible change. We designed the series to be used one part at a time, for small groups of men meeting together for a couple of hours each week. (By small groups, I mean somewhere between two and twelve guys.) It can be used in larger settings, too, and I'll explain how in a moment.

If you plow straight through, you could obviously do it in eight weeks. We typically allow for some great conversations, throw in a few movie clips of our own, linger on one or two parts that seem to have really touched a nerve or that have raised a lot of questions. If you allow for that, it will take you maybe ten sessions to complete. At that point, you'll have a group of men on your hands that we believe will be "ruined" for anything other than the true kingdom of God. They'll want more. They'll want to hang together as a band of brothers and go deeper into the mission that God has for them. They will be well on their way to recovering their hearts, finding their places in the battle, learning to fight.

While this tool is best used in small groups, it can be used in other formats as well. If you have a large gathering of men coming together on a weekly basis, you simply adapt your format to start with the video, then break into small groups after showing the video to tackle the discussion points. Or if small group breakouts are not possible, you can use that time by having them do the *Field Manual* exercises in the larger setting, making the time a sort of seminar or workshop. Of course, we strongly encourage the use of small groups because forming bands of brothers is one of the key objectives.

This series can also be the backbone for a powerful men's retreat, where you use the video segments for your teaching times and then break into small groups or, as we do, send the men out for times of solitude and reflection with God. Here's how we use the material in a retreat setting:

Friday Night: Part 1
Saturday Morning: Parts 2 and 3
Saturday Late Afternoon: Part 4
Saturday Night: Parts 5 and 6
Sunday Morning: Parts 7 and 8

I'll make suggestions as we go along for those of you wanting to use it in that manner.

YOUR PART

As I said before, you don't need any experience leading men's groups to use this tool. But I think by the time you're finished, you'll feel like a leader. Remember, the story of God is the story of how he uses ordinary men and women to accomplish the extraordinary. "But, Lord, I'm just a boy, a common man, a fisherman, a sinner," is how every man reacts when God calls him. I hope you find that encouraging because God is going to use you to do something really amazing. In the following pages I have laid out for you a game plan for each session, including the goal for that session, the key Scriptures to focus on, recommended film clips to use as supplemental material, and a series of questions for group discussion.

The ideal approach would be to have each man read the corresponding chapter in *Wild at Heart* and do the work in the *Wild at Heart Field Manual* over the course of the week before your meeting. That way, they will be primed and ready to go when you meet. Of course, as facilitator, you should do the same. It would also be a good idea for you to watch the video for that week's session ahead of time and read through our recommended game plan. When you gather, you simply follow the plan we've laid out for the session. You light the fuse; God will do the rest.

One last word. Wild at Heart is not a fad. It's not simply the "next thing" to come down the parade of Christian products or events. What we have laid out here is simply the eternal gospel in words and images a man was meant to understand. Yes, this is a movement, a grassroots movement, a wildfire started by God and a few good men, and fanned into flame by his Spirit. This is a work of God. Listen to just a few of the comments from men who have been through our workshops:

"Against all hope that it could even be done, he has set me free."

"I am ruined for Christ. I have been pushed over the edge to a full-time life for Christ."

"This has been the greatest experience of my life. Because of y'all, I know a relationship with a validating heavenly Father that is deeper than I have ever known. I go now to the front line. You have taught me how to fight in the biggest battle ever."

"My heart is so healed and is held in the hands of Jesus."

"I have never felt closer to God. This has been the most powerful Christian experience of my life. Words don't do it justice. This is now my way of life."

"It was very hard for me to come to the conference—I had been taken out by the Enemy. I have been separated from my wife for six months. Now I am crying freedom and am fighting for my family, wife, and my Lord."

And my favorite comment of all:

"I came with a raised eyebrow and left with a new heart."

This video series and the guide you are holding are exactly what we use in our Wild at Heart retreats, workshops, and small groups. And so it should not surprise you to know that the Enemy fears it and opposes it in any way he can. Heads up. Be prepared for hassles, setbacks, opposition, and spiritual attack. You'll feel totally unprepared and unqualified for this. You'll hear accusations that it's going badly, that you're just not connecting with the men, that you're disqualified. It's all a lie, from the Father of Lies. Go back and reread Chapter 9 in *Wild at Heart*. And by all means, pray one of the daily prayers offered on pages 214–19 in the *Field Manual*. Take the attack as a backhanded compliment. The more opposition you encounter, the more assault you feel . . . well, then, you must be that dangerous!

When the troops heading for Normandy filed onto their transports and landing crafts, General Eisenhower gave them the Order of the Day. As you read his words, consider that they might also be the words of our Commander to you personally:

> Soldiers, Sailors, and Airmen of the Allied Expeditionary Force: You are about to embark upon the Great Crusade, toward which we have striven these many months . . . Your task will not be an easy one. Your enemy will fight savagely. But the tide has turned! The free men of the world are marching together to Victory! I have full confidence in your courage, devotion, and skill in battle. We will accept nothing less than full victory! Good luck! And let us beseech the blessing of Almighty God upon this great and noble undertaking.

Yes, this is a great and noble undertaking. As one woman wrote to me, "This country needs its men back!" And, yes, this is a work of God. It's good to know that he is far more committed to your success than you are. My prayers go with you.

John Eldredge
Colorado, November 2002

PART I

THE HEART OF A MAN

THE GOAL

Your objective for this opening session is pretty simple: to wake guys up.

Most men are totally distracted by the demands of their lives—work, the kids, bills to pay, all that. They live on the surface of life and rarely take a deeper look. This first session is designed to wake them up to the deep heart that God has put in them as men. To awaken the desires shared by every man, to help them put some words to those desires, and to validate those desires as good and true and God-given. That's all you're after in week one.

OPENING

We've found that a very powerful way to reach men is to use clips from films they are familiar with, movies they love. Better still are the trailers that studios create to advertise those films. They tell the story in a powerful way, in about three minutes, for general audiences (meaning, they're typically "safe" content). If you are using DVD, you'll find the trailers included in the "special features" section on most major motion pictures released on DVD. For the opening night of your gathering, show one of the trailers for *Braveheart* at the very top of your meeting time. Yep, I mean start with it. The guys come in, grab a cup of coffee, take a seat, and suddenly the lights are dimmed and you roll the trailer. This has two powerful effects. For one, men love it; it wakes them up. And two, it lets them know that this is going to be different from your average church gathering. Something inside them will say, "Hey, this is going to be *good!*"

You don't have to use the film clips to make this a powerful experience. The video series itself will do that. But, from years of leading groups and retreats for men, I can tell you, the clips are a really good addition, a launching point. You're going to need all the equipment anyway—go for it. (And allow me to state the obvious: it would be good if you watched the entire film, in advance, for each of the clips. That way you're in a better position to set it up, and explain it.)

YOUR INTRODUCTION

After the trailer I typically get up and react to it, say a few words about what it stirs in me. Put the men at ease. Welcome them. Set the stage for your time together by laying out a vision. Here is why we're getting together, here is how many weeks we'll meet, for how long each week. Tell them that it's an eight-part series, that your plan is to watch one part each week, do some work in the *Field Manual*, and talk about it. Most important, tell them *your* desire for them, why you've called them together. Tell them what's on your heart.

Don't preach. Don't start with, "We aren't the men God made us to be, and it's time we stop fooling around and get serious about being *men!*" Don't scare them off by saying, "We're going to get really honest here, guys. We're going to get *vulnerable* and share the deepest secrets of our lives." Say something like, "Hey, I think there's a whole lot more that God wanted for us as men, and somehow it's gotten lost along the way, and I'd like to take a journey with you guys and see if we can get it back. *Wild at Heart* has really struck a chord with several of us, and I think you are going to love this. I love the line in *Braveheart:* 'All men die; few men ever really live.' We're here to come alive as men. To really begin to live."

Should you open with prayer? Worship? Well, that's your call, but let me offer a warning: you don't want this to feel like Sunday school. Meaning, you don't want this to feel "religious." You want these men to open up, be honest, be themselves. In the weeks to come, you are going to ask them to talk about some pretty raw places in their lives, to "get real." Sadly, most guys put on a mask at church when they feel they're supposed to be "spiritual" or "good boys." Compare what it's like to watch the Super Bowl at your buddy's house or hang out together watching a movie with the way guys act at church. You want the feel of these meetings to be far more like their "real" world. I think the opening should disarm them a bit, make them feel that this is going to be real.

ROLL THE VIDEO

We live in a very media-savvy culture. Most of these guys go to the movies and have great sound systems in their cars and/or homes. *Don't ruin this by using old or second-rate equipment.* You're doing a video series, after all. The impact of the media needs to be strong, so use a large screen and a great sound system. Believe me, we've been doing this with men for years, and the investment in good equipment is worth it. *Don't trust the church to have what you need.* I've had it happen too many times. I call ahead, and the church secretary says, "Oh, yes, we have everything you need. Our sound man will make sure of it." And I get there, and what they have is a twelve-inch TV from 1972 and lousy sound. *Check the equipment ahead of time, personally.* That way, if it's not top rate, you can beg, borrow, or rent what you need.

What do you need? A thirty-inch TV hooked up to a stereo system works for a group up to about fifteen guys. For larger gatherings, you'll need a video projector of at least 2,000 lumens that you *know* your DVD player works with (because you've tested it) and at least a ten-by-twelve screen. Don't compromise. You'll also need a good sound system you can patch your player into for audio. Don't rely on the speaker that is included in the projector. It stinks.

DO THE EXERCISES

After you roll the video, turn the lights back on, and have the guys pull out their *Field Manuals*. Now, the plan is to have them do their homework ahead of time each week by reading the chapter in *Wild at Heart* and doing the corresponding chapter in the *Field Manual*. However, the memory span of most guys is about twenty-two minutes. Take them back into a couple of the key questions each week to refresh their memories and prime the pump for the discussion time. Of course, in this first week they won't have done anything because now is the time for you to hand out the *Field Manual*s.

Have them turn to page 10 and answer the last three questions, starting with the one about favorite movies. Encourage them to use the blank page on the right. Give this ten minutes. We recommend you play some background music to set the mood, like the sound track from *Braveheart*. A silent room can feel awkward, like they're back in Mrs. Nagbuster's fourth-grade grammar class taking a test.

Then have them turn to page 26 and answer the first question, the one about what they feel pressure to be at home, work, and church. Resume the background music for another five minutes.

In a retreat format, we send the men out for an hour alone with God to work through the questions. It has been a very powerful part of their encounter with God.

TAKE A BREAK

My guess is, you've gone about an hour by this point, what with a late start and doing the exercises and all. Give the guys a restroom break, or you'll lose 'em during the most important part—the discussion time.

TALK ABOUT IT

Okay, I'm assuming that either you're in a small group, or you're going to ask the men to break into small groups at this point. It's almost impossible to have a meaningful discussion with a room of fifty men. Two or three guys will dominate, and the rest will sit there in the silence of Adam. Use small groups between six and ten guys.

I'm going to lay out a course for discussion. This is the second half of your time together, and I'd recommend you give this an hour each week. This can be the most powerful part of the experience, processing what they are discovering. The questions I recommend are only a guide. Trust your instincts. If you feel you want to head in another direction, go for it. Before I suggest the questions to run with, let me offer some advice on facilitating small groups:

- Start with less-personal questions. Men aren't used to talking about their lives, their dreams, and their desires. Help them get used to small group discussion by leading off each week with "soft balls," easy-to-answer questions. Then progressively move to the harder issues.
- Lead by example. This is a very personal journey. When it does come to the more vulnerable questions, I suggest you go first. Don't dominate the time, but let your vulnerability create a safe place for theirs. "Here's how I pose," or "Let me share with you my wound."

Stay focused. You can't possibly cover all the material in the *Field Manual* during your discussion time. Pick a handful of questions, and stay focused on them. I'll make recommendations for each week. You may not even get through the questions I recommend. But you certainly won't make headway if you let the conversation wander. Keep it on track with kind but firm direction.

- Deal with the nonstop talker. Inevitably, some groups are going to wind up with a man who wants to dominate the conversation, take it off track, and talk about his life for an hour—or simply a guy who can't make a point in under thirty minutes. With love and firmness, you will need to cut him off when it becomes apparent that he is going on and on. Say something on the order of "Jim, excuse me, but our time is running short and I know you want the other guys to have a chance to talk tonight, so please finish your thoughts in just a sentence or two."

- Shut down the doctrine cop. No doubt at some point you'll encounter a guy who doesn't really want to learn from this series; he wants to make a doctrinal point or take a stand or pick a fight. You'll want to shut that down, too. With kind firmness, say something on the order of "You know, Jim, this just isn't the right format for holding a theological debate or trying to sort through our doctrinal differences. We respect your convictions, but we ask you to respect ours as well. Tonight, we're focusing on [whatever the topic is], and I'm going to have to end this so we can get back on track."

- Help the broken man. As you move forward in the series, and especially as you hit the subject of the wound, you may encounter a man who is so deeply broken, he starts to fall apart in the group. You want to love him, but you also don't want to let him take over the rest of the night. Don't turn the group time into a counseling session for one man. You may need to pause and pray for him, ask God to meet him in his deep need. Affirm him. If it becomes apparent that he wants a sort of group therapy session week after week, you'll need to take him aside and recommend he see a trained counselor. I'll make specific recommendations for the week you cover the wound.

- Ground rules: I think it's important to lay down a couple of ground rules for small groups the very first time you gather. Don't be heavy, and don't come down on them or make it sound legalistic. Just state a few simple rules. (1) *Confidentiality*. Every man agrees that nothing gets passed along outside the group. What's shared in the group stays in the group. Break this rule and you're out. (2) *No teaching*. There are many gifted guys, and some of them will be tempted to take the stand and begin teaching the others. Make it clear that we're here to listen and ask questions. (3) *Respect the men by not trying to "fix" each other or offer advice*. As a man shares something from his story, listen well. Ask questions. Affirm him. But don't tell him how to live his life. Don't offer advice *unless he asks for it*.

Okay, now for the discussion questions for Part 1. If you're working with a number of small-group leaders, you'll want to copy these and pass them along.

1. Start with the favorite movies question. Ask each guy to share a couple of his and *why* he loves those movies. This is usually a great discussion starter. It's a "safe" question and gets the blood going, too. Now, heads up—95 percent of the guys are going to name movies that fit the direction of this series: *Top Gun, High Noon, Rocky, Gladiator*. But some clown is going to try to be funny by naming *Dumb & Dumber* or *Caddyshack* or something like that. Just laugh along

with him, but don't let him derail the discussion. Get it back on track by turning to another man and asking him what his favorites are. Make sure you share yours.

After each guy has had a chance to speak, point out that most of the films they mentioned have one or two or all three of the core desires of a man's soul: a battle to fight, an adventure to live, a beauty to rescue. Help them make the connection.

2. Then go back around and ask them who they'd like to be, the character they'd love to play in those movies. This is a little more personal, but hardly like getting undressed. Guys usually run with it, and it will give you a great insight into each man. I try to remember (or write down in my manual) the character each man mentions. It will come in handy for later discussions.

3. Now turn to boyhood. Use the video as examples. "Craig talked about the neighborhood he grew up in, how they loved to play army, defend the neighborhood with tangerine grenades and popguns they could push in the mud and fire dirt clods with." (This is a very effective technique, to remind them of the way we talked with each other in the video and what we talked about.) Ask them what games they played as boys, what adventures they loved to have. You might have to prime the pump by sharing a few of yours, but be brief. You don't want to dominate the group or let any man go on and on about his life.

4. Now anchor this in Scripture. Reread Genesis 1:26–28, and ask them if they ever realized that the way we bear God's image is at the level of gender. "Was that a new thought for you?" could be a good question. But a warning: every now and then a group gets a doctrine Nazi—a guy who's got some theological ax to grind. Don't let him take over the group. If he disagrees, point out that the Scripture does not say, "So God created people." It says, "So God created man in his own image . . . *male and female* he created them." Remind him that God does not have a body—he is a spiritual being—and so the image we bear can't be physical. It must be spiritual. We bear God's image, that image is a spiritual, not a physical, image, and it is as a man or as a woman that we bear the image. Gender, therefore, is spiritual, soulful, eternal. If he still doesn't want to accept this, move on by saying, "Well, you've clearly got your position on this issue, Bill, and we're not going to turn this into a theological debate, so let's move on."

5. Now turn from what they *want* to what they have actually *lived*. Point out that "John mentioned in the video that most men give up on those core desires for battle and adventure and beauty. Or as William Wallace says in *Braveheart*, 'All men die; few men ever really live.' Has life encouraged you to live from your heart, to live out those desires? How did you answer the question on page 26?"

6. "Craig talked about being like his horse—nose in the rear end of the guy ahead, staying in line, playing it safe. Can you relate to that?"

7. "John asked the guys a pretty basic question: 'What is it you want to be known as, as a man?' Gary said he wanted people to say, 'Gary was strong and wise and discerning.' Bart wanted to be remembered as courageous—that he had what it takes when it was time to come through. John said he wanted people to say that 'he fought well and because of his life I'm free.' What is it for you? How would you answer the question 'What do you want to be known as, as a man?' Is it to be the sweetest guy ever? The nicest guy?" You might have to go first if they can't put this into words or if they've never even thought about it.

8. "John quoted Proverbs 4:23: 'Watch over your heart with all diligence, for from it flows

the wellspring of life' (NASB). He went on to say that *desire* is what starts a man on his journey and what sustains him on the way. He's not saying that every desire that occurs to us is good. Sometimes we have sinful desires. But not every desire is sinful. In Psalm 37:4 King David prayed that God would give us the desires of our hearts. Those desires we share for battle and adventure and beauty are God-given. So, how would you finish the sentence, 'For the rest of my life I want to _____'? Craig said he wanted to live with freedom and passion. Morgan said he wanted to first discover who he is and then live with abandon and courage. What about you? How would you finish the sentence, 'For the rest of my life I want to _____'?"

Again, you'll want to have a good answer ahead of time to help guide them in theirs. Some joker might say, "I just want to make a lot of money." Share yours, something like, "I want to be a man, a real man. I want to fight for my wife and kids. I want to live an adventure that God has for me."

WRAP UP

You'll want your close to be strong. First, remind the group that next week you'll be doing Part 2, and they need to read Chapter 3 in the book (urge them to reread it if they've read it before) and do the work in Chapter 3 in the *Field Manual*. Then you'll want to remind them of the key points from tonight:

- God made us in his image, as men. He set within every one of us a masculine heart.
- If we are ever going to find the life we were meant to live, we've got to get that heart back.
- That's why we're here. That's the journey we're going to take together.

Close with a prayer like this:

> *Jesus, thank you for this opportunity to discover what it means to be men, to recover the man you made us to be, to find the life you meant for us to live. We ask you to come for us, to take us on this journey. We give you permission to raise the deep issues of our hearts and our lives. We ask you to meet us here. Over this next week, help us hang with it. Take us into the work, and help us find you there. We ask this in the power of your name. Amen.*

And an exhortation like this:

> Be on your guard; stand firm in the faith; be men of courage; be strong. Do everything in love. (1 Cor. 16:13–14)

PART 2

THE POSER

THE GOAL

Your objective for session two is a little bit tougher: to help your guys face up to the poser that they are or, at least, the poser they sometimes play.

Our experience is that about half the guys are going to be right there with you, ready to admit they pose. And about half are going to act "clueless" so that they don't have to admit they are a poser. Some will even deny that they do pose. That's like saying, "I have no sin," which, as John pointed out, is a lie (1 John 1:8). However, your objective is *not* to get every man to own up to being a poser. That's impossible. Your goal is simply to offer an opportunity for them to own up to being a poser. Whether they take the opportunity or not is their decision.

OPENING

I'd start week two by welcoming the men back and setting up your time together by saying something like, "Okay. This week is a little tougher. This week we're going to face the poser. In case you're still not clear on what a poser is, I want to show a scene from a very funny movie." There's a very funny and clear picture of a royal poser in the movie *Groundhog Day*, starring Bill Murray. Bill plays a self-centered weatherman named Phil Connors who finds himself trapped in a sort of time warp on Groundhog Day. He's forced to live the same day over and over again. About halfway through the movie he's trying to pick up the producer of the newscast in a bar. Over and over he tries to "get it right," to fake his way into her life. (On the DVD it's in Chapter 18, at the time code 46:10.) When we use the scene, we show it all the way through their dinner together in the German pub, when he fakes knowing French poetry. The scene always cracks guys up and exposes them at the same time.

When the clip is over, make a transition from *Groundhog Day* to the *Wild at Heart* video series Part 2. React to Bill Murray. Tell the guys you know exactly what that's like. (The more honest you are about the way you pose, the better chance they'll own up to theirs.) Get them warmed up. "Okay, there's a picture of a real poser. Now you know what John and the team are talking about as we watch Part 2."

ROLL THE VIDEO

Okay. I'm going to say it again. *Don't ruin this by using lousy equipment.*

If you are doing this in a retreat format, we take a short break after showing Part 2 (on

Saturday morning) and return to watch Part 3 as well. Then we send them out to do both sets of exercises over about an hour.

DO THE EXERCISES

After you roll the video, have the men pull out their *Field Manual*s. Tell them you know that some of them have done the work and some of them haven't. Even those who have done the exercises in the *Field Manual* need a refresher (the memory span of most guys is shorter than a seventh-inning stretch).

Have them turn to page 62 and answer the questions on that page. Acknowledge that "for many of you, this is review. But have another look at those questions and think again about your answers there." Give them fifteen minutes. I recommend you use new background music for week two, maybe the sound track from *Legends of the Fall*.

Again, if this is a retreat format, send them out to do the exercises from Part 2 and Part 3 in time alone with God. Give them an hour.

TAKE A BREAK

Give the guys a restroom break.

TALK ABOUT IT

At the start of your small-group discussion time, I'd remind everyone of the ground rules: "Hey, guys, just a reminder . . ." You won't need to do this, of course, if you are meeting with a group of men you know well and trust. But new groups need a reminder as they learn the ropes of being together.

1. Start by going back to what we were doing in the video—rappelling off a 100-foot cliff. Ask the guys as a warm-up question what they thought about that: Would *they* want to step backward off a 100-foot cliff?

2. "Last week we talked about how we are made in the image of God to fight great battles, take great adventures, rescue the beauty. Tonight in the video John asked the guys if that's how they feel *inside*, most of the time. Several of them admitted feeling fear, feeling that they don't know what to do, and afraid to ask. Do you feel bold and daring and strong inside on most days? Or more uncertain, fearful, hesitant?"

3. Read Genesis 3:1–10, then ask them the first of two vital questions. First, have they thought about Adam's sin like that—that he was right there, and he said nothing, did nothing? He was paralyzed and silent. "Can you relate? Where in your life do you feel Adam's sin? Where do you feel afraid to speak up or to take action?" (If they have a hard time with our interpretation of the passage, because most men have been told that Adam was not there, point out the Hebrew for the phrase "her husband, *who was with her*" means right there, elbow to elbow. "With her" means very close at hand.)

4. Lead up to the second question by saying, "Adam is afraid, so he goes into hiding. John said, 'What you meet when you meet a man is an elaborate fig leaf; what we call our person-

ality can sometimes be a brilliant disguise.' Bart said he was hiding in business because he feared he didn't really understand all the answers, so what he wanted the world to see on the outside was a successful developer on top of everything. Gary said that the way he hides in situations where he doesn't know what to do or say is to get quiet and look wise. But all the while he's hoping nobody asks him to speak up. Craig admitted hiding through humor, being the funny guy. John hides by being the driven guy, the perfectionist. How are you hiding these days?"

5. Or, if they can't put words to it, ask them how they are feeling, right now, about sharing in the group. Use the fear of the moment. "I'm feeling nervous right now. I'm afraid you guys will think I'm a poser, trying to lead this group. That you'll discover I don't have what it takes. How about you? What are you afraid the group might discover about you?"

6. "Last week we talked about movies we love and the roles we'd love to play [remind them of the characters they chose]. That's the man we want to be, but is there a character that you fear you really *are*? Most guys want to be Wallace but fear they are Robert the Bruce. What character do you fear you might in fact be?"

7. "Where in your life are you aware of the question every man is asking: 'Have I got what it takes?' Is it at work? In your marriage? With your kids?"

8. "John said the poser is created out of our fear. That we, just like Adam, are afraid we aren't what we should be. So we hide behind the poser. The poser comes out of the question 'Have I got what it takes?' and we pose because we don't think we do. John talked about the fear of taking on your boss on a tough issue, or initiating sex with your wife, or talking to your eighteen-year-old daughter about her life. Where have you felt that question come up in your life? Where have you felt like, 'Whoa . . . do I have what it takes to do *that*?'"

9. Ask them to share from page 66 in the *Field Manual*. "How do you see yourself as a man? Are words like *strong, passionate,* and *dangerous* words you would choose? What did you put down?"

10. "Do you think that's what the people in your life would say? What do you fear *they* would say as they describe you as a man? What words do you think they would use?"

11. "Toward the end of the video, John said that God comes to all of us as he came to Adam, calling to us, asking us to come out of hiding. To face our fears, to walk with him into our true strength. John said he felt God was asking him to stop trying to control everything. Gary said he's being asked to speak up, jump into situations where he doesn't have a plan. Where is God calling you out of hiding? What are the cliffs you need to step off of?"

WRAP UP

Again, you'll want your close to be strong. Remind the group of the key points from tonight:

- We are all sons of Adam. All of us have created a way of hiding: the poser.
- Every man has a question. Every man shares the exact same question: "Have I got what it takes?"
- The poser is created out of the fear that we don't have what it takes. And the poser is in the way. There is no moving forward in our journey until we are honest about the way we've been hiding, faking our way through life.

- We will not discover the real weight of our lives until we leave the poser behind.

Close with a prayer like this:

> *Jesus, help us to be honest about ourselves and the way we, like Adam, have gone into hiding. Help us to see the ways that fear is shaping our lives. Again, we ask you to come for us, to take us on this journey. We give you permission to raise the deep issues of our hearts and our lives. We ask you to meet us here. Over this next week, help us hang with it. Take us into the work, and help us find you there. Show us where you are calling to us, asking us to come out of hiding. And give us the strength and courage to follow you. We ask it in the power of your name. Amen.*

And an exhortation like this:

> Be on your guard; stand firm in the faith; be men of courage; be strong.
> Do everything in love. (1 Cor. 16:13–14)

(You might want to use the same exhortation or benediction each week. Make it kind of a theme for the group.)

Remind them that next week you'll be talking about the wound. They need to read Chapter 4 in the book (urge them to reread it if they've read it before) and do the work in Chapter 4 in the *Field Manual*.

PART 3

THE WOUND

THE GOAL

Your objective for session three is even tougher: to help your guys face their wound.

The objective is *not* to push all the way through to healing the wound. That comes next week. This week, you are taking them into their wound. Again, our experience is that about half the guys are going to be right there with you; they know they've been wounded. And about half are going to act "clueless" so they don't have to face their wound. Some will even deny they have a wound. Your mission is *not* to get every man to admit a wound. Your goal is simply to offer an opportunity for them to face it, see it, put words to it. Whether they take the opportunity or not is their decision.

OPENING

Welcome the men back. If you're in a small group setting, check with each other. "How's your week been?" Set up your time together this week by admitting right up front, "This week is a tough one. The wound is not an easy topic to go into." Then offer some encouragement right up front by reminding them, "The point of going into our wound is to be able to live from a whole heart, to see God heal us and set us free. There's no way around this one. We have to head through it together."

Then I'd set up the film clip for this week, which comes from Disney's movie *The Kid*. The scene we use comes toward the end of the movie. Russell Duritz (played by Bruce Willis) has just turned forty. He's in a major midlife crisis. He hates his job; he has no friends; he has no life. He's a jerk. The story line is that little Russell, his eight-year-old self, shows up one day to take him on a journey to get his heart back. The climax of the film is when big Russell remembers the day he received his wound. (On the DVD, it's scene 20.) Sometimes what we'll do is start with scene 1, the top of the movie, to give guys a picture of what big Russell is like. It's a great reminder of the poser. After about five minutes of that, we go on to explain, "The poser is never the deepest thing about a man. The poser comes out of our fear, and our fear comes out of our wound. Let me show you why he became that man." And then we show scene 20. You don't have to do this; scene 20 by itself is very powerful.

TRANSITION

You'll need to transition between *The Kid* and the video. It's a tearjerker of a scene they just saw. Say so. React to it. Then read Isaiah 61:1–3. Remind the men that the mission of Jesus Christ, described in this passage, is to heal our hearts and set them free. Tell them, "Facing the wound is tough, but it's worth it. Now let's listen to the stories of John and his band of brothers."

ROLL THE VIDEO

If you are doing this in a retreat format, remember what I told you earlier. We take a short break after showing Part 2 (on Saturday morning) and return to watch Part 3 as well. Then we send them out to do both sets of exercises over about an hour.

DO THE EXERCISES

After you roll the video, have the men pull out their *Field Manuals* and turn to page 92. Read aloud what I wrote there in "A Break in the Clouds." Then have them answer the first two questions on that page. Acknowledge that "for many of you, this is review. But have another look at those questions, and think again about your answers there." Give them fifteen minutes. The background music we use for this is something sober, not "happy." We use Samuel Barber's Adagio for Strings No. 2; it's in the sound track for the movie *Platoon*.

However—if you are in a well-oiled small group, and the guys really are doing the work each week, then skip this part and jump straight to the conversation (after giving them a quick break).

TAKE A BREAK

Give the guys a restroom break.

TALK ABOUT IT

At the start of your small-group discussion time, I'd start with some counsel. "Talking about our wounds can be pretty tough. Let's respect one another by listening and not offering advice, or trying to fix somebody's wound. Let the weight of it be what it is. Each of us has a story to tell."

1. I'd start by reading aloud two Scriptures: Psalm 109:21–22 and Psalm 27:10.

2. "This week, our conversation is going to be a little different. We need to allow some more time for each man to tell us part of his story, so we can hear about each other's wounds." Then lead the way by telling them about yours. Include some details, tell a story, but try to get it said in about twelve minutes. That will set the example for the group, as will our stories from the video.

Then simply ask, "Who's next? Who'd like to tell us about your wound?" It's better to let each man volunteer than to go around the group, point to a man, and say, "Now it's your turn." Typically, this is going to take up your whole discussion time. In fact, you may need to allow a second week to hear every man's story. Do it. It's worth it.

If a man really begins to break down as he speaks (or as another speaks), pause and let his tears flow. Don't try to put a quick Band-Aid on it. Grief is good. Tears are good. Tell him that. Let him weep. Ask a few brothers to pray for him, over him. Let it subside, and then move on with the encouragement that "this is not the end of our journey. We talk about the wound so that we can let God heal it. The journey gets better from here." Some gentle word like that.

3. If every man does tell his story, and there's more time left (I'll be surprised if there is, at least in the first week you give to this), ask them, "What was your dad's *message* to you in answer to your question 'Do I have what it takes?' What did your dad teach you about yourself as a man? John said the message for him was, 'You're on your own.' Craig said it was, 'You're nothing but a seagull. You have nothing to offer.' Gary realized the day they were filming this that his message was, 'If you can't get it right, then I don't want to be with you.' What was your dad's message to you?"

4. However, there are times when guys either rip through their wound story or report that they haven't yet discovered their wound. Sometimes a man will report that he can't remember a father-wound, but he does have another wound he'd like to talk about. Fine. Let him tell that story.

If the men are having a hard time identifying their wound, take it a different direction. Ask them about the conversation we had in the video at lunch, on the rocks, when we talked about what we did with our dads. "What was your relationship with your dad like when you were a boy? What kind of stuff did you do together?"

5. If they still aren't clear on what their wound is, have them turn to page 98 and do the "One Final Question" exercise.

IF YOU NEED MORE TIME

Listening to the stories of each other's wounds is a crucial part of this journey. Don't rush through it. You may very well need another week. Take it. Devote next week to the wound. Tell the guys who have not shared to make sure they are ready to share next week. Remind the group to do Chapter 4 in the *Field Manual* if they haven't, and to go on and do Chapter 6 in the *Field Manual* if they have. That will help them carry on the journey.

My game plan for a second week on the wound is nearly the same as for this week. I would show the scene from *The Kid* again next time as a way of getting them back into the rawness of their wound. (Or you could show another "wound" scene from a different movie. There's one in *The Rookie*.) Carry on with the storytelling. Then if you have some time left, ask every man to respond to question 3 above.

WRAP UP

Your wrap-up is crucial. Don't try to quickly sweep it all under the rug. Don't offer platitudes about "all things work together for good." Acknowledge how hard it is to go into the wound, and thank them for their honesty. Make it clear:

- Every man carries a wound.
- The wound nearly always comes from the father (or the lack of a father).
- The wound strikes at our deepest question—"Do I have what it takes?"—and the wound always says "no."
- We can't get our hearts back until God heals the wound that each of us carries.

Then pray,

> *Jesus, come and meet us here. Come to us in our woundedness, and minister your grace to us. We ask that you would do in us the very thing you promised to do: to heal our broken hearts and set them free. Help us stay with this and not sweep it under the rug. Help us face our wound with deep honesty. Show us this week how our wound has shaped us all our lives. We ask it in your mighty name. Amen.*

Remind them that as the Scriptures say, "weeping may last for the night, but a shout of joy comes in the morning" (Ps. 30:5 NASB). Tell them your plan (if you have truly finished and every man has spoken about his wound) is to move on to Chapter 7 in the book and *Field Manual*: "Healing the Wound." Encourage them to read the chapter and do the work in the manual.

PART 4

HEALING THE WOUND

THE GOAL

Now for the good news. The objective for session four is: to help bring the healing of Christ to the wounds of your men.

Your part is to usher them into the healing of God; it is not your responsibility to heal them. That's God's part, the core of Christ's mission as foretold in Isaiah 61:

> The Spirit of the Sovereign LORD is on me,
> > because the LORD has anointed me
> > to preach good news to the poor.
> He has sent me to bind up the brokenhearted,
> > to proclaim freedom for the captives
> > and release from darkness for the prisoners. (v. 1)

The reason that I've come, Jesus says, is to bind up and heal your wounds, and set your heart free. This is *the* central passage in the entire Bible about Jesus, the one he chooses to quote about himself when he steps into the spotlight in Luke 4 and announces his arrival. What you're going to do is invite your men to take Jesus at his word—asking him in to heal their wounds.

OPENING

Welcome the men back. Check in with one another. Many of them will probably have had a pretty rough week, opening up the wound. Some may already have stories to tell, from their work in the *Field Manual*, of how God has begun to heal them. Let them tell their stories; hearing those stories will encourage the others.

There are two choices for film clips you might want to use. One is *The Legend of Bagger Vance;* the other is *Good Will Hunting*. As I mentioned in Chapter 7 of the book, there is a beautiful picture in *Good Will Hunting* of what can happen when a man realizes he has "owned" his wound and discovers he doesn't have to. Will Hunting (played by Matt Damon) is the brilliant young man who works as a janitor at MIT. No one knows about his gift because he hides it behind a false self of "tough kid from the wrong side of the tracks." He's a fighter (a violent man). That false self was born out of a father-wound. He doesn't know his birth father. The man who was his foster father would come home drunk and beat Will. Will is ordered by a judge to see a psychologist, Sean (played by Robin Williams). They form a bond; for the first time in Will's life, an older man cares about him deeply. Toward the end of one of their last sessions, Sean and Will are talking about the beatings he endured, now recorded in his case file. Heads up—this scene has some rough language in it. I simply warn the guys about that (they've heard it all by now) and use this powerful scene (Chapter 17 in the DVD).

If you don't want to use the scene because of its language, we also use *The Legend of Bagger Vance* quite often. It's the story of a young man named Junuh (also played by Matt Damon) who was once a great golfer, but who lost his heart during WWI when all the men in his company were killed in combat. He was the captain of a company of men from his hometown, and he lost every one of them. Point out to the men in your introduction of the scene that when a man fails at the greatest mission of his life, the message is loud and clear: you do not have what it takes. That's a wound. Junuh became a shell of a man, falling into drinking and gambling—his way of hiding. Bagger Vance is a picture of the Holy Spirit, who comes to call Junuh out of hiding to regain his heart and his glory. Toward the end of the movie (Chapter 17 in the DVD, at the time code 98:32), Junuh has hit his ball off into the woods (a metaphor for a lost man). His fears come racing back to face him, and his wound is raw. Bagger sees him through.

TRANSITION

React to the movie. Share your thoughts about it, how it is a picture of Christ coming to heal us. Read again Isaiah 61:1. Remind the men that the mission of Jesus Christ, described in this passage, is to heal our hearts and set them free. "Let's listen to what John and the team have to say."

ROLL THE VIDEO

You know what to do with these, so I don't have to say anything else.

DO THE EXERCISES

After you roll the video, have the men pull out their *Field Manuals* and turn to page 126. Set up the exercise by reading this passage from *Wild at Heart:*

"Men are taught over and over when they are boys that a wound that hurts is shameful," notes Bly. "A wound that stops you from continuing to play is a girlish wound. He who is truly a man keeps walking, dragging his guts behind." . . . A man's not supposed to get hurt; he's certainly not supposed to let it really matter. We've seen too many movies where the good guy takes an arrow and just breaks it off, keeps on fighting; or maybe he gets shot but is still able to leap across a canyon and get the bad guys. And so most men minimize their wound. "It's not a big deal. Lots of people get hurt when they're young. I'm okay." . . .

Or perhaps they'll admit it happened, but deny it was a wound because they deserved it. After many months of counseling together about his wound, his vow, and how it was impossible to get The Answer from women, I asked Dave a simple question: "What would it take to convince you that you are a man?" "Nothing," he said. "Nothing can convince me." We sat in silence as tears ran down my cheeks. "You've embraced the wound, haven't you, Dave? You've owned its message as final. You think your father was right about you." "Yes," he said, without any sign of emotion at all. I went home and wept—for Dave, and for so many other men I know and for myself because I realized that I, too, had embraced my wound and ever since just tried to get on with life. Suck it up, as the saying goes . . .

God is fiercely committed to you, to the restoration and release of your masculine heart. But a wound that goes unacknowledged and unwept is a wound that cannot heal. A wound you've embraced is a wound that cannot heal. A wound you think you deserved is a wound that cannot heal. That is why Brennan Manning says, "The spiritual life begins with the acceptance of our wounded self."

Ask them to choose one of the ways I've listed that men mishandle their wound. And ask them to write down why—why did they choose that way of handling their wound? Give them ten minutes. You might want to use background music again that's sober, not "happy." To repeat Samuel Barber's Adagio for Strings No. 2 (from the sound track for *Platoon*) would not be a bad idea.

If you are doing this in a retreat format, we do "Healing the Wound" on Saturday afternoon. Don't send them out until you've prayed through the healing prayers listed below. Then send them out for an hour to be with God.

TAKE A BREAK

Give the guys a restroom break.

TALK ABOUT IT

1. You might start your discussion time by saying, "What we're after tonight is the healing of our wound. As John wrote in the *Field Manual*, 'The way in which God heals our wound is a deeply personal process. For one man it happens in a dramatic moment; for another, it takes place over time. Even after we've experienced some real healing, God will often take us back again, a year or two later, for a deeper work of healing.'"

You can say something like this: "Just so we're all back on the same page again, let's each describe our wound again. Maybe God has shown you more this week, too. Tell us about that."

2. "Before we can go to healing, we have to start with what we *have* done with our wounds. John said that most men mishandle their wound. We deny that it exists, we minimize it, or we actually embrace it and the message as true. John said he thought if he ran fast enough and hard enough, he could put it behind him. Craig said what he did was to try to prove it wrong. Gary said he embraced it. He just figured the message was true—that no one wants to be with him unless he has his act together, so that's what he tried to do—get his act together. How have you handled your wound over the years? What have you done with it?"

3. "John said we still have a question. It does not go away. It rules us whether we're aware of it or not because we still crave that validation, the words and affirmation that we need. Do I have what it takes? Am I a real man? Where are you going for validation? What are you looking to? John said if we're scared to talk to our wives, then we're looking to them for validation. We don't want to get an F so we stay away. So many young men take their question to the woman. Bart went looking for validation at work, and though a big win felt great, it lasted about a day because you've got to do it again and again and again. Where are you going for validation? And is it working?"

4. "What would you love God to say to you, about yourself, as a man?"

5. At this point in your discussion, I'm hoping that the men are aware of their wound, feeling it to some degree and craving that validation they still need. Before your time is up, it would be good to lead them through the healing prayers given on pages 146–58 of the *Field Manual*. What I mean is that you invite the men to take Christ up on his offer.

"What I want to do now, as a group, is to pray through those healing prayers John gave us in the *Field Manual*. I think it would be good for us to pray through them together, to take Jesus up on his offer, and to ask him to come and heal our masculine souls, to heal our wounds. What we're going to do is this: I'm going to pray out loud, and I want you to follow along with me through each prayer, agreeing with me in your hearts. Let this be real for you. Mean it."

To make it simpler for you, I've consolidated those prayers right here.

"It begins with surrender; we give ourselves fully to God:

> *Dear Jesus, I am yours. You have ransomed me with your own life, bought me with your own blood. Forgive me for all my years of independence—all my striving, all my retreating, all my self-centeredness and self-determination. I give myself back to you—all of me. I give my body to you as a living sacrifice. I give my soul to you as well—my desperate search for life and love and validation, all my self-protecting, all those parts in me I like and all those I do not like. I give to you my spirit also, to be restored in union with you, for as the Scripture says, "He who unites himself with the Lord is one spirit with him." Forgive me, cleanse me, take me and make me utterly yours.*

"And we invite Christ into our wound. We give him permission and access to our wounded hearts:

> *Jesus, take me into my wound. I give you permission and access to my soul and to my deepest hurts. Come, and bring me to my own brokenness. Come and shepherd the orphaned*

boy within me. Let me be fully present to my wounded heart. Uncover my wound, and meet me there.

"And we renounce any vows we've made, and the ways we've mishandled our wound:

Jesus, I renounce every vow I've made to seal off my wound and protect myself from further pain. Reveal to me what those vows were. I break every agreement I have made with the lies that came with my wounds, the lies of Satan, and I make all agreement with you, Jesus. I give the protection of my heart and soul back to you; I trust you with all that is within me.

"And we ask Christ to do what he promised to do—heal us, set us free:

And precious Jesus, I invite you into the wounded places of my heart, give you permission to enter every broken place, every young and orphaned part of me. Come, dear Lord, and meet me there. Bind up my heart as you promised to do; heal me and make my heart whole and healthy. Release my heart from every form of captivity and from every form of bondage. Restore and set free my heart, my soul, my mind, and my strength. Help me to mourn, and comfort me as I do. Grant my soul that noble crown of strength instead of ashes; anoint me with the oil of gladness in every grieving part; grant me a garment of praise in place of a spirit of despair. O come to me, Jesus, and surround me with your healing presence. Restore me through union with you.

Father, strengthen me with your true strength, by your Spirit in my innermost being, so that Jesus may live intimately in my heart. Let me be rooted and grounded in love, so that I, too, with all your precious saints, may know the fullness of the love of Jesus for me—its height and depth, its length and breadth. Let me be filled with real knowing of your love—even though I will never fully reason it or comprehend it—so that I might be filled with all the life and power you have for me. Do this in me, beyond all that I am able to ask or imagine.

Jesus, I choose to forgive my father for all the pain and all the wounds he gave to me. It was wrong, it hurt me deeply, and I choose now to pardon him, because your sacrifice on the cross was enough to pay for these sins. I release my father to you. I also release any bitterness I've harbored toward him, and I ask you to come and cleanse these wounds and heal them.

"Finally, we ask God to father us, to validate us, to tell us our true names:

Father, who am I to you? You are my true Father—my Creator, my Redeemer, and my Sustainer. You know the man you had in mind when you made me. You know my true name. O Father, I ask you to speak to me, to reveal to me my true strength and my real name. Open my eyes that I might see, give me ears to hear your voice. Father, I ask that you speak it not once, but again and again so that I might really receive it. And grant me the courage to receive what you say and the faith to believe it. I ask all this in Jesus' name. Amen.

"Now, we're just going to linger here in silent prayer before God, listening prayer, and ask him to speak to us even now."

Do just that. Linger in silence about five minutes (it will feel like twenty if this is new for your guys). Let God move. Let him speak.

6.   "This is just a beginning. God will come and will heal. But we need to let him. As John said, the hardest part about hearing God validate us, hearing his new name for us, is letting it be true. Craig heard, 'You do have something to offer. You do have a role to play. You are a warrior shepherd for my kingdom.' Bart heard, 'You have a strength that's yet to be revealed.' Has God spoken to you about your new name yet? What's that been like?"

7.   "The masculine journey comes alive, and we take our biggest step into the frontier when we ask God to father us. Remember what Bart discovered, that he realized he hadn't been fathered since he lost his dad, and he asked God to come and pick up where his dad left off. God wants to initiate us. He wants to tell us our true names, tell us what we need to hear. But he also wants to take us through a series of initiations where we can discover who we really are as men, and that we do have what it takes. How has God done that for you?"

WRAP UP

"This is the first part of your mission for this week—to stay with the Question until you get an answer from God. Look for his words to you in surprising ways: a song on the radio, a movie that you love, a Scripture that jumps off the page at you. And listen for his voice. *Take time to do this, just as the guys did in the video.* Get away for several hours with God.

"We're going to move on next week to 'A Battle to Fight,' so you'll want to read Chapters 8 and 9 in *Wild at Heart,* and get as far into the *Field Manual* as you can.

> *Father, once again we ask you to come and father us. Initiate us as your sons. Speak to us, Father, again and again, so that we might know it is you. Tell us who we are. Initiate us into masculine strength. Heal our wounds and set our hearts free. We stand together as one man against our Enemy, and we bind Satan from lying to any man, from accusing, from wounding us again. Jesus, protect us in your authority and in your name. Amen.*

PART 5

A BATTLE TO FIGHT

THE GOAL

Your objective for session five is: to rouse the warrior heart in your men, affirm it, and get them into the battle—starting with the battle for their own hearts.

OPENING

Welcome the men back. Check in with one another. Ask them if they have a story to tell about God "fathering" them or giving them a new name this past week.

The film clip I'd recommend for this week comes from *Braveheart*. The scene is right before the Battle of Stirling (Chapter 10 on the DVD). As I described it in the book,

> When Wallace arrives on the scene, Scotland has been under the iron fist of English monarchs for centuries. The latest king is the worst of them all—Edward the Longshanks. A ruthless oppressor, Longshanks has devastated Scotland, killing her sons and raping her daughters. The Scottish nobles, supposed protectors of their flock, have instead piled heavy burdens on the backs of the people while they line their own purses by cutting deals with Longshanks. Wallace is the first to defy the English oppressors. Outraged, Longshanks sends his armies to the field of Stirling to crush the rebellion. The highlanders come down, in scores of hundreds and thousands. It's time for a showdown. But the nobles, cowards all, don't want a fight. They want a treaty with England that will buy them more lands and power. They are typical Pharisees, bureaucrats . . . religious administrators.
>
> Without a leader to follow, the Scots begin to lose heart. One by one, then in larger numbers, they start to flee. At that moment Wallace rides in with his band of warriors, blue war paint on their faces, ready for battle.

Or another really great scene is found in *The Matrix*. It's the showdown in the subway scene, where Neo finally takes on the Enemy (it's scene 33 on the DVD). What's so powerful about this scene is that it is a direct battle with Satan, who is the Accuser (Rev. 12:10), and the way Neo wins is through the power of his "new name." He knows who he is. Sometimes I will show *both* clips, showing *Braveheart* to open and *The Matrix* scene at the end of our session as the wrap-up. It makes a lot of sense at that point.

TRANSITION

React to the movie. Ask the guys, "Why couldn't the nobles rally their men?" Then ask them, "What does Wallace do? How is he able to give those men back their hearts?"

(The nobles know only about cowardice and compromise. Wallace gives the men an identity, a new name—he calls them Sons of Scotland. Then he calls them up into a much larger story. He gives them a part in a great battle. Just like Jesus, he says, "He who seeks to save his life shall lose it; but he who loses his life will find it.")

ROLL THE VIDEO

DO THE EXERCISES

"Turn to page 198 in the *Field Manual,* and answer all three questions" (the first question actually starts on the bottom of page 196). Give them fifteen minutes. How about the sound track to *Gladiator* as background music?

If you're doing this in a retreat format, you're going to also show Part 6 tonight (Saturday night). Have them do these exercises right there in their seats. Take a short break, then do Part 6.

TAKE A BREAK

Give the guys a restroom break.

TALK ABOUT IT

1. "Think back again to some of your favorite movies. Do they have a battle in them? What battle does the hero have to face?"

2. "Have you seen Jesus as being a great warrior? What *are* your images of Jesus?"

3. "John pointed out the story from Luke 13—how Jesus didn't hesitate to take on the hypocrisy of the Pharisees. He *humiliated* his opponents. He turned tables over in the temple. In fact, we need to remember that the God of the Old Testament is the same as the God of the New Testament. They aren't two different people. The Exodus. Jericho. Gideon. King David. 'The LORD is a warrior; yes, the LORD is his name!' [Ex. 15:3 NLT]. What does that stir in you?"

4. Read Revelation 19:11–21 out loud. Then ask, "So, is Jesus more like William Wallace or Mother Teresa?"

5. "God, who is a great warrior, creates man in his image. As John said, 'God set within us a warrior heart because he has created men to join him in his war against evil, and if we're going to find our part in God's story, if we're going to be the men that he made us to be, we have to

get that part of our heart back.' Has life encouraged you to be a warrior? Let's start with your boyhood. Did your parents let you play with guns? Were you encouraged to be fierce?"

6. "And what about nowadays, as a grown-up, and as a Christian—do you think that aggression is a good thing? Are you encouraged to be fierce?"

7. (This is optional; you want to make sure you get to questions 9 and 10 tonight.) "What do you think Jesus meant when he said, 'The kingdom of heaven suffers violence, and the violent take it by force' (Matt. 11:12 NKJV)?"

"And how does that relate to Adam's sin of silence and paralysis? Can you see that to be passive is to be like Adam in his sin, and to be aggressive is to be like Jesus?"

8. "A man needs a battle to fight. Without a great battle, a great cause to give ourselves to, we battle for the smallest things. What would you say is your biggest battle right now in your life?"

9. "What about spiritual warfare? The Bible makes it clear—we are in a spiritual war. 'Put on the whole armor of God' (Eph. 6:11 NKJV). 'Resist the devil' (James 4:7 NKJV). And how about 1 Peter 5:8–9: 'Be self-controlled and alert. Your enemy the devil prowls around like a roaring lion looking for someone to devour. Resist him, standing firm in the faith, because you know that your brothers throughout the world are undergoing the same kind of sufferings'? Has spiritual warfare been part of your Christian life? Why, or why not?"

10. "John said Satan's first strategy is simply 'I'm not here.' Can you relate to that? Can you see how he'd love to blame you or God for everything he's causing? John warned us that the first battle we're going to have to fight is for our own hearts—fighting shame, and discouragement, and accusation. Can you see that happening to you as we do this series? How has the enemy been attacking your heart?"

11. "Okay. What will you do to fight back? As they said in the video, 'We must begin to see life as an assault against our heart and against the image of God in us.' We must begin to resist, to fight back. What will you do?"

WRAP UP

- God is a warrior. And he made us warriors in his image.
- We were born into a world at war. We are created to join God in his battle against evil.
- Our first battle is for our own hearts. Winning the battle for our hearts starts with the truth about a *new* heart. Review the teaching from the Scriptures on pages 176–78 in the *Field Manual*. You have a new heart. Your heart is good. All the accusations are from the Father of Lies. Resist him! Fight for your heart!

"Next week we'll cover 'An Adventure to Live,' so jump ahead to Chapter 11 in the book and the *Field Manual*.

"Let's close by praying together the Daily Prayer John gave us on pages 217–19 of the *Field Manual* [or you can choose another]."

PART 6

AN ADVENTURE TO LIVE

THE GOAL

Your objective for session six is: to rouse the adventure heart in your men, and help them see and embrace the risks God is asking them to take.

OPENING

Welcome the men back. Check in with one another. Ask them how the battle has been this past week. Let a few guys tell a story.

The film clip I'd recommend for this week is the airplane scene from *Never Cry Wolf*, which I talked about in the book:

> Canadian biologist Farley Mowat had a dream of studying wolves in their native habitat, out in the wilds of Alaska. The book *Never Cry Wolf* is based on that lonely research expedition. In the film version Mowat's character is a bookworm named Tyler who has never so much as been camping. He hires a crazy old Alaskan bush pilot named Rosie Little to get him and all his equipment into the remote Blackstone Valley in the dead of winter. Flying in Little's single-engine Cessna over some of the most beautiful, rugged, and dangerous wilderness in the world, Little pries Tyler for the secret to his mission.

It's a riot, and it makes a great point. You'll find the scene on the DVD at Chapter 3.

TRANSITION

React to the movie.

ROLL THE VIDEO

DO THE EXERCISES

"Turn to page 250 in the Field Manual, and answer the question under the heading 'Asking the Right Question.'" Tell them to go on and answer the questions on page 252 as well. Give them ten minutes. How about the sound track to *Last of the Mohicans* as background music?

TAKE A BREAK

Give the guys a restroom break.

TALK ABOUT IT

1. "How about the white-water rafting—should we do something like that as a group? What would you guys love to do?" (Plan an adventure together!)

2. "The guys talked about the Bible as one adventure story after another—Abraham leaving it all to follow God, Jonah, Peter walking on the water. Has Christianity felt like a great adventure to you? On a scale of 1 to 10 (with 10 being the highest), how exciting is your life?"

3. "John said that the false self, the poser, is usually built as a way of controlling our lives, our way of reducing risk. How much risk would you say you've taken in the last couple of years? Are you taking risks to follow God, or are you playing it safe?"

4. "Let's come back to that statement John used: 'Don't ask yourself what the world needs; ask yourself what makes you come alive, and go do that. Because what the world needs are men who have come alive.' I think that needs some more clarification because it's a crucial idea and it gets misunderstood.

"First, not every desire that occurs to us is good. Paul says in Romans 8:5 that we have sinful desires, and we have desires stirred in us by the Spirit of God. John's not saying just go do whatever you desire. However, some of our desires, our deepest desires, are put there by God.

"What John is saying is that the deep calling of our lives, the reason God made us, our 'life purpose,' is written into our heart's desires. Paul wanted to preach the gospel. It was his desire, and it was his calling. David wanted to be God's chosen king. (Read 'From the Map' on page 256 of the *Field Manual*.) It was his desire and his calling. Craig wants to be a warrior shepherd. His desire is his calling. Gary talked about the story of leaving his job of fifteen years because he no longer really cared about sports or evangelism. It wasn't his desire anymore. God had something new for him.

"So, let's go there. What are the deep dreams of your life? What are your true desires for your life? Don't ask *how*. Just ask *what*. What makes you come alive?"

(Facilitator, this one question should take you the rest of the night! Let the guys dream, talk about their lives. It takes time. Let desire arise. A good follow-up question would be: "What were your favorite movies? What roles did you want to play?" And, "Has God spoken to you yet about your new name?" Those two issues will almost always connect to their dreams and their calling. Sometimes it's a huge revelation to "connect those dots" for a man. One of my favorite movies is *Braveheart*. One of the new names God has given me is "Wallace." And my calling is to fight for the freedom of God's people . . . to set their hearts free. See how it works?)

5. "And what's keeping you from living your dreams? What act of faith would it require to begin to follow your dream? John talked about how all this almost didn't happen. He had to take a huge risk to leave Washington and go to grad school, but his dream was to write and speak and go after the hearts of men. He took the risk, and look what's happened. There's a revolution taking place around *Wild at Heart*. What act of faith would it require of you to begin to follow your dream?"

WRAP UP

- Adventure is a deeply spiritual longing that God put in every man.
- Not all adventures are equal. The biggest adventures occur when we follow God.
- The point about adventure and risk-taking is this: it reveals what we think of God. When we do not risk, we are saying, "God, I don't trust you." God made us for adventure. He made us to trust him.

Jesus, we ask you to open our eyes that we might see where you are calling us into an adventure. At work, at home, here with each other—show us, Jesus, the adventure you have for us. Reveal to us how our life's calling is written on the desires of our heart. Make it clear to us, Lord. Remove the fog. Give us clarity, and give us courage to follow you. In your name. Amen.

PART 7

A BEAUTY TO RESCUE

THE GOAL

Your objective for session seven is: to rouse in your men their desire to rescue the beauty, affirm it, and get them into the battle for her.

OPENING

Welcome the men back. Check in with one another.

The film clip I'd recommend for this week comes from the recent movie version of *Les Misérables* (starring Liam Neeson). There are other "rescuing the beauty" scenes, like the one in *First Knight* where Lancelot rescues Guinevere, but this one is so poignant because he not only sets her free, he heals her wound by speaking to a woman's deepest question, "Am I lovely?" (It's scene 11 on the DVD.) You *must* show the scene all the way through the line where Jean Valjean says to Fantine, "You are his creation. In his eyes you are an innocent and beautiful woman."

TRANSITION

React to the movie. Point out how fierce Jean Valjean was—fierce love. He was like a lion (the Lion of Judah). Point out how he spoke to her wound, her deepest question.

You might also want to say something along the lines of, "Now, although we're using marriage as the example, all this applies to you single guys as well. You are made to pursue a woman. And all of us are called to fight for the heart of God's beauty, the church. So there is always someone in our lives we are to be fighting for."

ROLL THE VIDEO

DO THE EXERCISES

Tell the single men to turn to page 110 in the *Field Manual* and answer the questions about taking their question to Eve. Have the married men turn to page 236 in the *Field Manual* and begin with the questions under "Your Part in the Wound." Tell them to go on to page 238 and answer the first two questions there. Give them fifteen minutes. How about the sound track to *Titanic* as background music?

TAKE A BREAK

Give the guys a restroom break.

TALK ABOUT IT

1. "I think it's crucial for us to begin with the heart of Eve. Do you have a better idea now of what a woman longs for? What are the core desires of a woman's heart?" (Yes, you want them to say "to be fought for," "to be pursued," "to be part of a great adventure," "to be the beauty," and some of the phrases the women used in the video.) "Let's go around the group and name those core desires."

2. "What did it feel like to listen to those women talk about what a woman longs for? What did that stir in you? Did it help you understand? Did you think of your wife, or the woman in your life? Did it make you think about your failures?"

3. "Going on a bit more about Eve, how does she get wounded? What is a woman's deepest question, and what is her wound? What were the wounds that Tannah, Cherie, and Lori described?"

4. "Can you see the wound of a woman's heart in your wife, or in the women you know?"

5. "The guys were pretty honest in their feeling about wanting to fight for her . . . and not wanting to fight for her. Can you see now the sin of Adam at work in your life when it comes to fighting for Eve? Adam didn't speak; he was silent. He didn't move; he didn't act on her behalf. John talked about the day he came home and the boys were playing outside, Stasi was in a bad mood, and the door was locked. Everything in him said, 'Run away.' How have you been silent or passive, running from the hard places? How has that hurt your relationship with women over the years?"

6. "Before we can really go and fight for her, we have to be honest about the ways we've been taking our Question to the woman. Are you aware of how you've done that over the years? How you might be doing it even now?" (If they aren't aware, point out that if you are afraid to talk to your wife on an intimate level, if you fear her remarks or her criticism, then you are taking your Question to her. Also, if you find some woman irresistible, if pornography has had a pull on you, then you are taking your Question to her.)

7. "Okay, this is the toughest question of all: How have you added to her wound? Do you know what your woman's wound is—and if not, what does that say about how much you've fought for her?" (If they have no clue, ask them, "How have you been answering her Question then? In what ways have you spoken to her heart's deepest need?" If they still are clueless, ask them, "Okay. Are you willing to go home and ask her? I mean it—ask her whether you've helped to heal her heart or harden it. Ask her if she feels that you've really fought for her. Ask her if she feels pursued. What stirs in you as I tell you to do that?")

8. "The women talked about wanting to be part of the adventure, to play a crucial role.

How can you invite your women into an adventure?" (Of course, they first have know what their adventure is!)

9. "So, where do you see you need to move toward your woman? What do you need to do now to fight for her? Gary talked about taking dance lessons with his wife. What is it for you?"

10. "And what about your daughters? What do you need to do now to go after their hearts, speak what they need to hear?"

WRAP UP

- Every woman carries a wound, just as every man does. Her wound says, "You're not lovely. You're not worth fighting for. No man will really pursue you."
- God gave us this warrior heart to fight for Eve. It is essential to true masculinity.
- The woman is not supposed to be the adventure; rather, we are to invite her up into a great adventure. Don't leave her behind.

Jesus, forgive us for the ways we have failed the women in our lives, for the ways we have sought our validation from them. Help us see it clearly. Show us where we are acting like Adam—silent, passive, fearful to help the woman. Give us a deep repentance. Help each of us to see the heart of the woman in his life and go for it. Help us heal her wound, love her deeply as you love us. And call us both up into your adventure for us. We ask it in the power of your name. Amen.

"Next week is our last week. Do Chapter 12 in the *Field Manual*. And I want you to pray this week about where God might be calling us as a band of brothers. Where would you like to go from here?"

PART 8

A BAND OF BROTHERS

THE GOAL

Your two objectives for session eight are: (1) to recall and celebrate what God has done in your lives through this, to put it into words, drive a stake in the ground; and (2) to move together now into the future as a band of brothers, to make a plan for the next season you will spend together.

This is the closing session . . . but it's not intended to be the end. Far from it. One of the main objectives of this series is to bind men together into little platoons, bands of brothers. We are not meant to walk alone. We need one another. A band of brothers has two purposes: (1) to fight for one another's hearts, as we all fight the battle, live the adventure, and rescue the beauty; and (2) to seek God for the mission he may have for the band itself.

Much of where you go from here depends on how close your group has become. Some groups are very close. For you, I would recommend not only choosing one of the options I suggest below as your next series, but I would also seek God for the mission he may have for you as a band of brothers. Maybe it's to start a midnight basketball league for troubled teens. Maybe it's to take your wives, as a group, on a romantic getaway. Maybe he wants you now to offer this *Wild at Heart* experience to other men. If so, plan a men's retreat, or another eight-week series, and invite men in!

If your group is just beginning to come together as a band, I think you ought to at least covenant together to do another eight weeks, this time with another series. I have three ideas. One is to get together and watch the HBO series *Band of Brothers* (based on the book by Stephen Ambrose). It's the amazing true story of Easy Company of the 101st Airborne during WWII, all the way from their training to Normandy to the end of the war. What these guys went through and how they bonded make an incredible story. We've watched it as a band of brothers, and now we own it. It's available on DVD. Watch a part each week, and talk about it. After all the work you've done here, you will see so much, there will be many masculine themes to talk about!

A second thought would be to get together for another eight weeks and watch some of the significant movies for men, then talk about them. Again, your work here will open your eyes to many themes in those movies. There will be plenty to talk about! You could use the films I've recommended clips from, or come up with a list of your own as a group.

Last, it would be very powerful to do *The Journey of Desire Journal and Guidebook* together.

Journey is the book I wrote before *Wild at Heart*. It picks up on a lot of these themes, but goes deeper into desire (obviously) and how it leads us to the life God meant for us. It could be done as a twelve-week study if you went chapter by chapter. There is not a video series for it (yet), but what you could do is use the book and workbook as you've done here, and pick your own film clips for each week. Craig and I recommend some in *The Journey of Desire Journal and Guidebook*, which we wrote together.

If you do continue together, you might want to take a two- or three-week break between this series and your next.

OPENING

Welcome the men back. Check in with one another.

There are two possible film clips I'd recommend for this week. The first comes from the movie *Gladiator*. Maximus is "the general who became a slave, the slave who became a gladiator, the gladiator who defied an empire." Midway through the movie he and his little band of gladiator slaves have been brought to Rome. They are facing their first battle in the Coliseum. Standing alone together, they wait for the gates to open and an unknown enemy to appear. They know the odds are stacked against them. Maximus says, "Whatever comes through those gates, we've got a better chance of survival if we stick together. If we work together, we survive." You'll find the scene on Chapter XV (15) on the DVD. The scene gets a little violent, so I usually show it through just the first couple of attacks by the chariots, which demonstrates that as they lock their shields "as one," they win.

Another very powerful scene comes at the end of *Braveheart*. Wallace has been betrayed into the hands of the enemy, and he is tortured and crucified—just like Jesus. Every man who watches this scene is brought to tears. Most of them have never made the Christ connection. Just as important, after his death the men rally together and win the day on the fields at Bannockburn. You *must* show this scene through the end of the movie. That last image, of the small band of brothers charging the field, is the point you want to make. It starts at Chapter 20 on the DVD (I usually begin at time code 157:22, when Wallace is being brought in).

TRANSITION

React to the movie. Point out the band of brothers theme. You might make a few comments like, "Very few men ever find that in their lives. We tend to live alone, as men. And that's a very dangerous way to live. God intended us to live life with the help of others. To live in bands of brothers that fight for one another, just like that."

ROLL THE VIDEO

DO THE EXERCISES

Actually, there are no official exercises for this week. What you want to do is suggest a question for them to think about for a few minutes: "Where would you like to go from here as a group? Do you want to continue? What would you love to do? And, as you jot a few thoughts down, ask God what he wants for us."

TAKE A BREAK

Give the guys a restroom break.

TALK ABOUT IT

1. Start with this question: "We've taken quite a journey together over these past eight weeks. It's had its ups and downs for sure. What has God done in your life through this series, the *Field Manual*, and our time together?" I hope by now, they have some stories to tell!

2. "What's been the most meaningful part of this for you? What part would you say God most used in your life?"

3. "Over the last eight weeks we've watched John, Gary, Morgan, Craig, and Bart live together. They've rafted together, rappelled together, fished together. They made dinner for their wives. They've talked about life and their wounds and their dreams. Has that stirred anything in you? Do you want something like that in your life?"

4. "Why is it so uncommon for men to have close friendships? Why is a band of brothers—like the one John has—so rare?"

5. "John and the guys talked about how so many accountability groups or fellowship groups actually stay pretty superficial. Why is that? What makes a real band of brothers different?"

6. Share your idea to continue with them. Offer the thought of sticking together for another eight or ten weeks and taking on another series like the HBO *Band of Brothers* or another workbook like *The Journey of Desire*. Ask, "Would you guys want to move forward together? What would you like to do?"

7. If your band *is* intimate and bonded together, talk about what God might be calling you to do, as a band of brothers, for others. It's important to point out that the *first* mission of every band is to fight for one another's hearts. Meet regularly to do that. But, in addition, God may have a calling for your band. Talk about that.

WRAP UP

Ask the guys to close in prayer—to give thanks for all God has done, and to ask him to initiate you as men into the future.

And by way of closing, let me (John) say, I'm proud of you. This took guts. Not every man could have done this. Now stick with it. As I wrote in the introduction, *Wild at Heart* is not a fad. It's not simply the "next thing" to come down the parade of Christian products or events. What we have laid out here is simply the eternal gospel, in words and images a man was meant to understand. Yes, this is a movement, a grassroots movement, a wildfire started by God and a few good men, and fanned into flame by his Spirit. This is a work of God. *Stay with it.* Don't just walk away from all you've learned here. I've been through this series more than ten times, and every time I learn more. I am more alive and strong as a man now than when I first wrote *Wild at Heart*. God continues to speak to me as a man. Stay with the masculine journey. Review your notes. And above all else, ask God to father you, to initiate you, and then watch for his movement in your life.

ABOUT THE AUTHOR

JOHN ELDREDGE is an author, counselor, and lecturer. For twelve years he was a writer and speaker for Focus on the Family, most recently serving on the faculty of the Focus on the Family Institute. Now John is director of Ransomed Heart™ Ministries, a teaching, counseling, and discipling fellowship devoted to helping people recover and live from their deep heart. John lives in Colorado Springs with his wife, Stasi, and their three sons. He loves living in Colorado so he can pursue his other passions, including fly-fishing, mountain climbing, and exploring the waters of the West in his canoe.

To learn more about John's seminars, audiotapes, and other resources for the heart, visit his Web site, www.RansomedHeart.com, or write to:

Ransomed Heart™
P.O. Box 51065
Colorado Springs, CO 80949-1065

This *Wild at Heart Multimedia Facilitator's Kit* consists of four VHS videos or 3 DVDs, a leader's guide, in addition to the CBA Marketplace and Publisher's Weekly #1 best-seller *Wild at Heart* and the companion *Wild at Heart Field Manual*.

WILD AT HEART MULTIMEDIA
FACILITATOR'S KIT
ISBN 1-4002-0087-3 (VHS)
ISBN 1-4002-0086-5 (DVD)

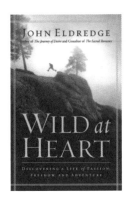

Every man was once a boy. And every little boy has dreams, big dreams. But what happens to those dreams when he grows up? In *Wild at Heart*, John Eldredge invites men to recover their masculine heart, defined in the image of a passionate God. And he invites women to discover the secret of a man's soul and to delight in the strength and wildness men were created to offer.

WILD AT HEART
ISBN 0-7852-6883-9

AUDIOS AVAILABLE APRIL 2003

Abridged Audio on 3 CDs—ISBN 0-7852-6298-9
Abridged Audio on 2 Cassettes—ISBN 0-7852-6498-1

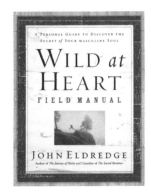

Abandoning the format of workbooks-as-you-know-them, the *Wild at Heart Field Manual* will take you on a journey throughout which John Eldredge gives you permission to be what God designed you to be—dangerous, passionate, alive, and free. Filled with questions, exercises, personal stories from readers, and wide-open writing spaces to record your "field notes," this book will lead you on a journey to discover the masculine heart that God gave you.

WILD AT HEART FIELD MANUAL
ISBN 0-7852-6574-0

Whether this special set is for yourself, to replace the dog-eared and penciled-in copies you already own, or is a gift to share John's powerful message with someone you love, these *Three Classics* from John Eldredge will continue to give long after they are received.

THE THREE CLASSICS:
THE SACRED ROMANCE, THE JOURNEY OF DESIRE,
AND WILD AT HEART
ISBN 0-7852-6635-6

This life-changing book has guided hundreds of thousands of readers from a busyness-based religion to a deeply felt relationship with the God who woos you. As you draw closer to God, you must choose to let go of other "less-wild lovers," such as perfectionistic drivenness and self-indulgence, and embark on your own journey to recover the lost life of your heart and with it the intimacy, beauty, and adventure of life with God.

THE SACRED ROMANCE
With Brent Curtis
Trade Paper Edition—ISBN 0-7852-7342-5
Special Collector's Edition (Hardcover)—ISBN 0-7852-6723-9
Abridged Audio—ISBN 0-7852-6786-7

The Sacred Romance Workbook and Journal is a guided journey of the heart featuring exercises, journaling, and the arts to usher you into an *experience*—the recovery of your heart and the discovery of your life as part of God's great romance.

THE SACRED ROMANCE WORKBOOK AND JOURNAL
ISBN 0-7852-6846-4

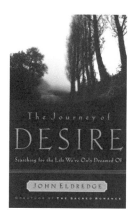

Author Dan Allender calls *The Journey of Desire* "a profound and winsome call to walk into the heart of God." This life-changing book picks up where *The Sacred Romance* leaves off and continues the journey. In it, John Eldredge invites you to abandon resignation, to rediscover your God-given desires, and to search again for the life you once dreamed of.

THE JOURNEY OF DESIRE
Hardcover Edition—ISBN 0-7852-6882-0
Trade Paper Edition—ISBN 0-7852-6716-6

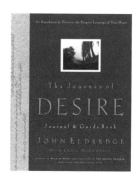

In *The Journey of Desire Journal and Guidebook*, John Eldredge, with Craig McConnell, offers a unique, thought-provoking, and life-recapturing workbook that invites you to rediscover your God-given desire and to search again for the life you once dreamed of. Less of a workbook and more of a flowing journal, this book elicits personal responses to questions from John and Craig.

THE JOURNEY OF DESIRE JOURNAL AND GUIDEBOOK
ISBN 0-7852-6640-2

Dare to Desire is the perfect book if you are ready to move beyond the daily grind to a life overflowing with adventure, beauty, and a God who loves you more passionately than you dared imagine. With brand-new content as well as concepts from *The Sacred Romance, The Journey of Desire,* and *Wild at Heart,* John Eldredge takes you on a majestic journey through the uncharted waters of the human heart.

DARE TO DESIRE
(Gift Book with Beautiful, Full-Color Design)
ISBN 0-8499-9591-4

❧ AVAILABLE JULY 2003 ❧

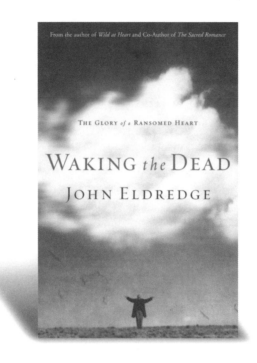

WAKING *the* DEAD
THE GLORY OF A RANSOMED HEART

There is a glory to life that most people—including believers—never see. In this insightful new book, John Eldredge presents the heart as central to life. Not only is the heart essential; the heart God has ransomed is also *good*. Building on these precious truths, Eldredge shows readers why real Christianity is a process of restoration, whereby the broken parts of our hearts are mended and captive parts are set free.

Hardcover—ISBN 0-7852-6553-8
Abridged Audio in 3 CDs—ISBN 0-7852-6299-7
Abridged Audio in 2 Cassettes—ISBN 0-7852-6380-2

THOMAS NELSON
PUBLISHERS
Since 1798